Zensho W. Kopp
Awakening to Your True Self

Zensho W. Kopp

Awakening to Your True Self

The Zen way of all-embracing mysticism

First edition October 2016

Translation: John Kitching
Cover design: Michel Schmidt
Back cover photo: Verena Kopp
Drawings: Zensho W. Kopp
Print optimisation: Reinhard Zanella
Typesetting: Torsten Zander

ISBN 978-3-751-931-82-3

Herstellung und Verlag:
BoD - Books on Demand, Norderstedt

Printed in Germany

Contents

The eternal self is never born,
nor does it ever die.
It comes from nowhere
and does not become anything.
Unborn, everlasting, immortal it is.
It does not die when the body dies.

Katha Upanishad

Introduction to the all-embracing Zen way

The true self, the original source of all life

The insatiable thirst for knowledge of our human nature has taken us far beyond the bounds of our planet earth into the universe. Yet all the while, we have sadly forgotten to discover ourselves. We are not seeking for our true essence but instead "something completely different", the reality behind everything, without realising that we can only find this within ourselves.

Due to this lack of understanding, we constantly try to reach lasting joy and contentedness in the external world, without realising that the source of all joy is constantly present within us as our true essence.

In the ignorance of our indwelling divine nature, caused by our spiritual blindness, we are so occupied with the matters of daily life that we have lost ourselves and no longer know who and what we are at the base of our being. Through this we have created a world without meaning, full of coldness and disappointment, and we have become entangled within in.

Thus, as long as our consciousness is primarily dominated by worldly interests and clings to them, it is not possible to realise our true essence and achieve freedom of the mind.

Most people are extremely stubborn when it comes to denying this unpleasant truth and cannot accept the deceptive nature of all phenomena and worldly activities – yet this is reality.

The Chinese Zen Master Yung-chia from the eighth century speaks the following admonishing words:

> The matter of life and death is immense and impermanence swiftly grasps hold. How can you waste your time with trivialities?

Yet we constantly try to avoid a confrontation with impermanence and would rather cling to the illusion of stability. We suppress the undeniable fact that death can come any moment and would rather believe that we have plenty of time before us.

By clinging to the notion of stability in life, our consciousness is so filled with thoughts and worldly matters that we have lost the connection to our innermost essential ground.

Thus, the main aim of this book is to turn our mental line of vision from its habitual external viewpoint to a viewpoint leading inwards. It places great emphasis on the Heart-Mind as our natural essence, in order to enable us to discover the reality of our true self within us. For it is absolutely impossible to find ourselves anywhere else than within ourselves.

The true and essential aim of our human existence is to reconnect with our true self as our innermost essence and to be anchored within in.

Therefore, it should be every person's greatest wish to experience the presence of his true, divine self within him. For it is the original source of all life, emanating from within itself, from out of which all life is brought forth in never-ending plenitude. We live and breathe it, without being aware of it.

The all-embracing wholeness of being

The key to perceiving our true essence and leading a meaningful life lies in returning to and becoming aware of this divine nature which we have forgotten. However, this perception is completely beyond all the possibilities of our intellectual understanding, for it arises from the depths of a direct, mystical experience.

Through this we reach a higher perspective and the truth reveals itself to us that we are constantly fulfilled, upheld and surrounded by an undivided, absolute Essence. The more we thus return to our true self, the more all distinctions and deceptions disappear and the deeper we experience the divine unity inherent in everything.

In this liberation from our limited, conditioned perspective, we will recognise more and more that our consciousness is no small consciousness, existing of itself. Instead, it is an all-embracing, birth- and deathless, boundless being, which contains everything within itself. We are a part of a boundless, cosmic reality and at the same time, in the depths of our being, the all-embracing wholeness itself. The question of our life's meaning is ultimately a question of our true self. It is the question of who and what we truly are at the base of our being. However, this can only be answered when, in mystical immersion in our innermost essential nature, we perceive our true self as the divine self common to all beings.

Wiesbaden, summer 2016   Zensho W. Kopp

Everything is the One Mind

1

Our original, divine nature

The omnipresence of the One Mind pervades the entire universe. All change and transformation is the continual self-evolvement and self-transformation of this Universal Mind. It is the self-realisation of the inexpressible divine ultimate ground.

Thus the whole unending multiplicity of the external world of phenomena is the manifestation of this one all-encompassing Mind, and the universe its revelation. This dynamic nature of the universe extends from the smallest atom to the vast dimensions of the galaxies. Everything is in never-ceasing motion, which ultimately takes place only in the mind. The mind is the fundament of everything, "out of it, through it and in it are all things," and beyond the mind there exists nothing at all.

The moment we turn our spiritual attention away from outward things, and in meditative clarity turn inwards, we will perceive that this One Mind is our true divine Self. In the darkness of the heart, in our innermost, it shines as a radiating light that lights up the entire universe like an eternal flame. This, our true being, is the underlying reality at the base of all our experiences. It is the true self, through which we live, feel and are aware, and allows us to experience the world. It neither comes nor goes, it is omnipresent, silent and pure, and beyond space and time. As the pure original source of all being it is unborn and indestructible, for it is the absolute essence; the ultimate, deepest meaning and reason of all life.

Yet, our original divine nature is constantly overlaid by a multitude of passions and notions. The perpetual flow of the incessant concept-producing intellect and our deeply-rooted thought-habits cast a dark shadow over our true Self.

Fascinated by this spectacle on the surface of our consciousness we are unable to free ourselves of it. And so we are in a state of darkness and confusion of the mind and are caught in our own projections. Blinded by this misperception, we are no longer able to perceive the reality of our true being, and thus we wander from incarnation to incarnation, lost in the ocean of suffering of Samsara, the cycle of birth and death. Trapped this way in the dream of an apparent world of multiplicity, we have lost ourselves and no longer know who we are at the base of our being. Yet since this dream-wandering is just a "vision", we cannot speak of a real occurrence in the sense of an actual event. We do indeed believe that we move in a three-dimensional, multitudinous world of space and time which exists separate from us – but in truth, everything takes place only in the mind.

In the Shraddhotpada Shastra, a Buddhist text from the second century, it is written:

> All things in the world are unreal and deceptive; they are no more than projections of the mind. Just like the reflections which appear in a mirror, in reality, all things too have no true substantiality; they are untrue, illusionary and "Only-Mind".

The mind-only teaching of Zen

What we generally deem to be the reality of our external world has in truth no more substance than a dream vision. In the words of the Chinese Zen Master Han-shan from the seventeenth century: The things of this world are just phenomena in a dream. When you awaken, the dreamer and the phenomena vanish.

> Whatever lives in a dream must also die with the dream; but behind the dream there is true being which does not cease with the dream.

Consequently, everything we perceive in the world, even the apparent solidness of substance is nothing other than the illusory notion of the mind. Our former thoughts and actions have created certain karmic tendencies within us which cause our mind to project this world that we now experience. That which we perceive as a solid, concrete external world is in reality, nothing more than the sum of events and objects of the perception, which are interlinked and dependent on one another. Everything is determined by a reciprocal interdependence.

This means that there is no independent existence. The world we live does not really exist, it is nothing more than a deception – a manifestation arising from our own mental formations.

However, if we believe we can infer the actual presence of an external world from our sensory perception of it, we are mistaken. The only proof we can provide here is the ability of our senses to function. Yet because our body and thus our senses too are just notions of the mind, this only proves that our consciousness experiences the impressions made by the senses.

Since we only perceive the world through our senses and consciousness, we must therefore concede that the only world we can speak of is the world of our subjective experience. And in the end this means: The world is nothing more than "our imagination".

An excellent example for the Mind-Only-Teaching is the following Zen story from the eighth century in China:

The temple flag above the great gate of the Zen monastery of the Sixth Patriarch Hui-neng is flapping in the wind. Two monks are standing beneath the flag arguing. One of them says, "Look how the flag moves." The other says, "No, it's the wind that moves." And so they discuss it back and forth and cannot agree.

Suddenly, the Sixth Patriarch is standing directly behind the two loud-ranting squabblers and says, "Neither the wind nor the flag moves. Only the mind moves, nothing else."

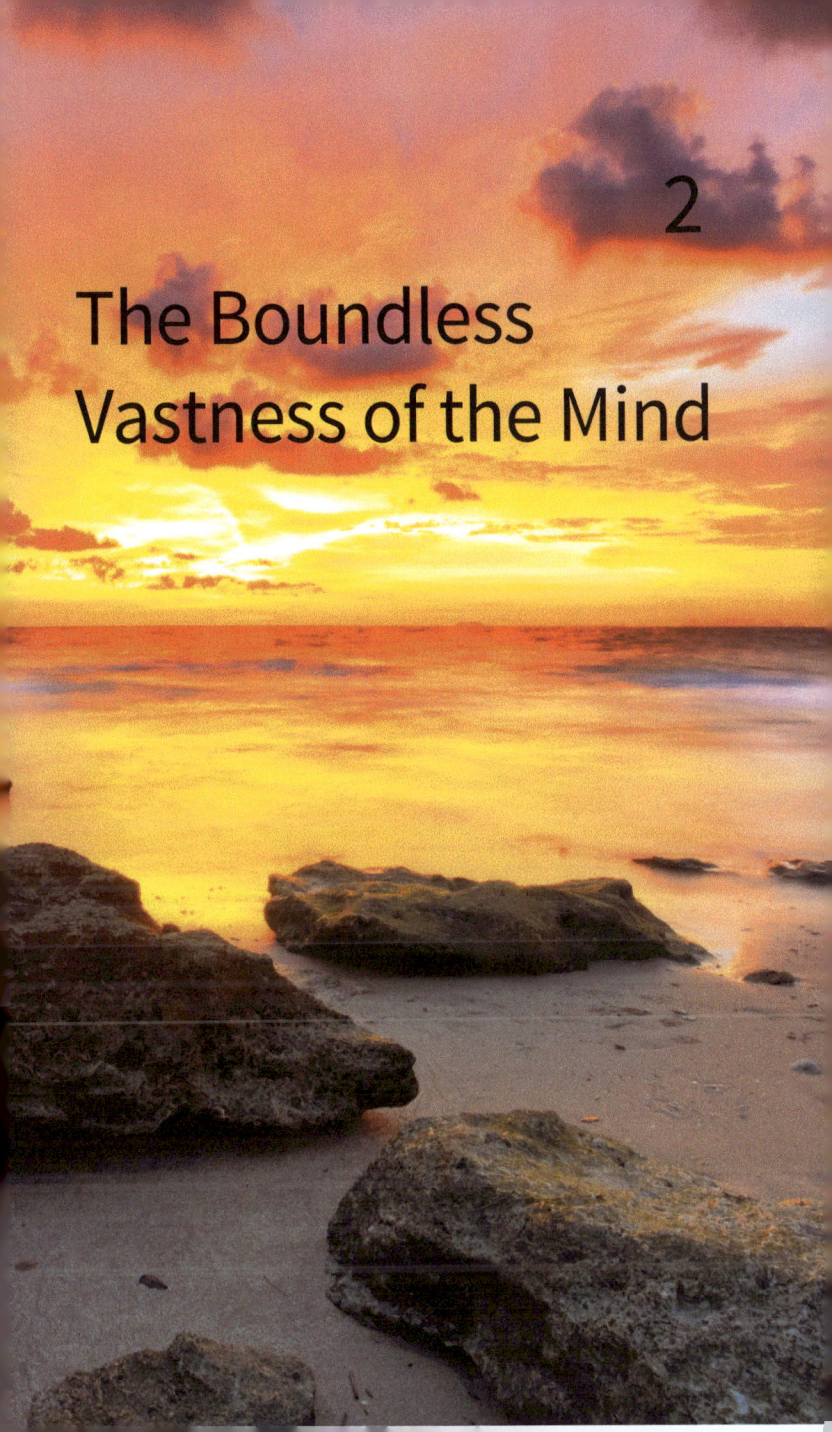

The Boundless
Vastness of the Mind

2

Contracted consciousness

Everything is the One Mind, beside which nothing exists. It is unending and all-pervading. In its absolute boundlessness it fills the entire universe with its radiance. By awakening from the dream of an external world of phenomena we will recognise that this One Mind is our true divine self and that there are no distinct, individual selves.

However, in our ignorance of this fact, caused by our spiritual blindness, we have created an artificial "I", together with the belief that we are an individual being, separate from all others. This erroneous ego-feeling covers our view of the reality of our true essence and is thus the real cause of our unknowing.

We do not know that at the base of our being we are the One Mind; the birth- and deathless reality. We have forgotten our original, true nature and live our lives in the identification with body, senses and intellect. In this way we have made ourselves slaves of the karma-law of birth and death. Ultimately, the individual self is nothing other than the "microcosmic partial aspect" of this all-encompassing One Mind, brought forth by dualistic and thus limiting thinking. The boundless expanse of the One Mind has thus been reduced to the small sphere of the individual consciousness.

It is as if we would look at the sky through a straw and would then take this very limited field of perception to be the whole sky. This is how we cling to our dualistic, constricted perspective as though it were the absolute truth.

We cling to our conditioned notions and move only within our self-made boundaries so that we take all that for impossible which is beyond our limited power of imagination.

In an old Indian parable, the situation of a person trapped in his limited perspective is compared to that of a frog in a well.

For a long time, a frog had been living in an old well down by the sea. He was born in it and grew up in it.

One day a fish, which by accident had jumped out of the sea, fell into the well. When the frog had recovered from his initial shock, he warily asked the newcomer: "What sort of strange creature are you and where on earth do you come from?" The fish replied, "I am a fish and come from the great sea." – "From the great sea?", the frog asked, most surprised. "So tell me, how big is this sea?" – "Very big," replied the fish. The frog stretched out his legs and asked, "Is the sea this big?" – "It is much bigger!" said the fish. Then the frog hopped with a great leap from one side of the well to the other: "Is it as big as this?"

"My friend," the fish answered, "the sea is so big that you cannot compare it to your well." – "Ha!", cried the frog, "now you've given yourself away, you liar, because nothing can be bigger than my well!"

In the dark shadow of Maya

As long as we cover our true being of the boundless transcendent Mind with all sorts of concepts and notions we are in this lamentable state of contracted consciousness. As a consequence, we are only able to perceive a tiny snippet, a diminutively small part of the whole reality.

In this state of contracted consciousness, a person is no longer aware of the universality of his mind. And so he lives a pitiful existence in the dark shadow of Maya – the great delusion of an apparent external world of phenomena.

Milarepa, one of the most important masters of Tibetan Buddhism from the twelfth century explains to us how we can liberate ourselves from this world of suffering:

> When a person's own mind recalls the original condition of his mind, all deceptive thoughts melt away by themselves in the realm of ultimate reality. Then there is no longer anyone who causes

suffering and no one who suffers. The most exhaustive study of the Buddhist scriptures teaches us no more than this.

If we seriously want to fathom the depths of all being, we must sacrifice all our beloved and familiar word-concepts and notions, and open ourselves to a new way of viewing things. Only then will we escape the enslavement caused by limiting, conceptual thinking.

As long as we are not prepared to take this step, we remain caught on the "finger which points to the moon", in the mistaken belief that the finger is the goal to which it points. In the Lankavatara Sutra, one of the principle texts of Mahayana Buddhism, it is written:

> When a person points to something, his finger might mistakenly be taken for the thing which is being pointed to. In the same way, the unknowing and naive are incapable of giving up the idea that the meaning itself is contained in a word.

Zen Master Hui-neng, the sixth patriarch of Zen from the

eighth century says of this:

> Those who know the meaning have gone past meaningless words and have transcended the letters. Whoever has gained this meaning forgets the words; he sees the root and leaves the teaching behind him.

3

Zen – Beyond Thinking

Instant perception of reality

It is an irrefutable fact that our habitual, logical way of thinking is incapable of understanding our original, true being and therefore the fundamental nature of all things. For this reason, Zen masters take no stock in abstract explanations and toilsome philosophical debates, which only ensnare us in the creeping tangle of logical dualism.

All philosophical and religious systems are a result of rational speculation. At best, one might grant these teachings an introductory, preparatory value. Yet in the eyes of the old Chinese Zen Masters like Lin-chi, Hui-neng and Yun-men, all the scriptures of traditional Buddhism are just worthless paper. The Chinese Zen Master Hung-jen from the seventh century tells us this too:

> Once we have perceived that the buddha-nature in all beings is as pure as the sun behind the clouds, we need only make effort to keep the fundamental, true mind completely clear so that the clouds of wandering thoughts dissipate and the sun of perception shines through.

What is the use of amassing great knowledge on the sufferings of birth and death, on all sorts of doctrines and principles and on past, present and future things? It is like wiping dust from a mirror; as soon as the dust has been completely removed, clarity shines of its own accord.

These words by Zen Master Hung-jen express the original, authentic Zen of the old masters. It is the pure form of Chinese Chan which will be spoken about in this book and which is radically different from the Zen Buddhism on offer nowadays.

The original, vivacious Zen of the old Chinese masters is the truth beyond all opposites. It stands out with its radical independence and cannot be understood through longwinded explanations and astute speculations. Zen is the truth of instant perception of reality and always points directly to the "Heart-Mind" – a person's true being. It is constantly of refreshing directness, without any frills, and thus a matter of pure experience. Like water running through our fingers, it eludes all conceptual denotation. Things are completely clear but they become unclear due to our discriminating, conceptual thinking.

Zen has but one goal: it wishes to thoroughly destroy all our attachment to words and our conditioned notions of body, mind and world so that we awaken from the dream of birth and death. It rises above all the logic of so-called common sense and directly addresses a person's spiritual intuition. That is why it remains incomprehensible and baffling for those who believe they can grasp Zen solely with their intellect.

But since we humans, in our blind trust in our intellect, always want to do everything with our heads, we have blocked our path to perceiving the truth beyond all words. Behind every answer we have found using our discriminating, conceptual thinking a new question arises, and the more we move towards the goal, the more we distance ourselves from it.

Liberation from compulsive thinking

In general, we have the tendency of asking seemingly plausible questions and then becoming inextricably embroiled in them. As long as we rely solely on our intellect we have no chance of escaping this vicious circle. For this reason Zen says:

> Leave everything behind you! Throw off your tainted, preconceived views and perceive things just as they are!

On the path to awakening to our birth- and deathless true self it is essentially about liberating ourselves from autonomous discriminating thinking, which like dark clouds, shrouds our true being. We could experience our true being right now in this instant, but we cannot because our consciousness is unable to abide in the present moment. Our thoughts are constantly drifting on, for we are always

on the run from the absolute present of Now. The inability to stop discriminating thought is a morbid state, in which a person inextricably entangles himself in the creeping snarl of concepts. Most people, however, cannot comprehend this and take this to be a normal state because everyone suffers from this illness.

In the powerful words of Zen Master Huang-po from the ninth century:

> All discriminating, conceptual thinking is a false opinion and the non-doubting of words is a woeful affliction.

But how can we free ourselves permanently from autonomous thinking? We cannot free ourselves by trying to suppress thinking by force; for every attempt to suppress thinking would only lead to a state of mental tension. Instead, freeing ourselves from thinking means releasing ourselves from the conditioned thinking-compulsion which darkens our true being. This takes place when we let go of the identification with the intellect – this being the cause of compulsive thinking – and by being absolutely present in Here and Now.

According to Zen teaching, the practice of true Zen meditation is therefore not about wilfully suppressing thoughts. Rather, it is about observing them without intention or reference, and judgement free, just as clouds passing by in the sky, for the arising thoughts are nothing more than projections of the ego-forming interwoven memories of our dead past.

In pure awareness of mind

When you are content with just observing the thoughts at the instant in which they arise and at the same time remain in pure awareness of mind, all mental unrest disappears and the empty intermediate state between thoughts expands. The Chinese Zen Master Pai-chang from the ninth century says of this:

If the mind digresses, do not follow it and the digressing mind will cease of its own accord. Should your mind wish to abide somewhere, do not follow it and do not abide there, and your mind's seeking for a place to abide will come to an end of its own accord.

In this way you come into possession of a non-abiding mind – a mind which remains in a state of non-abiding.

When you are completely aware of a non-abiding mind within you, you will discover that it is solely a matter of abiding, but nothing in which one could abide or not abide.

This perfect awareness of a non-abiding mind within you is known as "having a clear perception of one's own mind" or, to put it differently, "having a clear perception of one's true self".

Through the realisation of this presence-awareness, also known in Zen as "moment-awareness", we can break the power of the deceptive thoughts and all the concepts. When in an instant, all thinking suddenly ceases, we have reached the state of pure consciousness and can perceive directly to the heart of our radiant true being. In the absolute presence of Here and Now, the Eternal reveals itself. At this moment, right here at this place, the magnificence of Divine Being reveals itself. It lies neither in the past nor in the future. The highest truth is directly before us, now-here, nothing could be closer. Yet as soon as we think about it, we fall into delusion; we are here and there and thus we are completely outside reality.

If we were aware of the true nature of our birth- and deathless mind, we would recognise that the world of sense perception, including our intellectual reflections, only makes up a tiny fraction of reality.

We would realise that the moment we give up all arbitrary notions, endless and previously undreamt-of possibilities would open up to us, and the boundlessness of the universal consciousness would unfold before us.

4

The Search
for Happiness

Becoming aware of impermanence

Without knowing what we are actually seeking we strive for lasting happiness and wish to avoid suffering. Yet whatever joy life may bestow upon us, each moment of happiness, in fact everything we love is just short-lived in the end. And so we suffer, because through the force of habitual dualistic deception, we cling to impermanence and wish to keep hold of it.

In our illusion of lasting happiness we cling tightly to life. The ego binds itself to a life, limited by the ego-delusion, with its feeling of individuality. It wishes to give its pseudo-existence unlimited duration if it can, and to never die.

Yet this illusory life to which the ego clings is in fact nothing other than death since it separates us from our true, divine self. The more we are possessed in our spiritual blindness by the ego-delusion, the less is God present in us as the original source of all life. However, whoever has become aware of the impermanence of all worldly things and the suffering resulting from attachment to impermanence, reaches a higher perspective with inner disengagement from the things. He will no longer feel the desire to participate in meaningless activity like a hamster in its wheel. He has reached a level of clarity in which things have become clear to him that most people's attention just superficially glides over.

He has recognised that everything we achieve can never really give us satisfaction, for in fact, without knowing it, we are seeking something completely different. For this reason, the Christian Mystic Aurelius Augustinus from the fourth century says:

> Thou, O God, hast made us unto thyself, and thus are our hearts restless until they find their rest in thee.

Since everything we achieve can therefore give us no ultimate contentedness, we remain inwardly unfulfilled and set our sights ever higher. Yet every attempt to build lasting contentedness on the flighty, transitory joys of this world must finally end in disappointment.

We grasp at what we believe is gold, and in the end we have nothing but dry sand which runs through our fingers. We humans chase after happiness by trying to satisfy our wishes with all available means. When they are fulfilled, we are happy – when not, we are sad. Yet fatally, these wishes burn like a bushfire and demand ever more fuel.

Inner detachment

During most of our lives we are plagued by a specific or undefined desire for this or that, all for the sake of grasping a short moment of fleeting happiness. We have the tendency of confusing happiness with pleasure, without realising that pleasure is just an illusion – a shadow of happiness. Most of us spend their whole lives in this delusion, constantly on the lookout for new pleasures. Yet everything is fleeting and cannot bring us lasting, true happiness. Consequently, true happiness can only be found in the "Everlasting". It can only be found in that which is independent of space and time because the present is not tangible, the past is just a thought and the future equally so.

We cannot hold on to a moment in time without the past taking instant possession of it and turning it into a memory. Buddha describes the situation with these powerful words:

This world will come to pass and everything of importance dissolves to nothing. You must each awaken from your dream. There is no time to lose and thus: Be steadfast in your efforts! All existence is impermanent like autumn clouds. Like scenes from a play are birth and death on the stage of life. Like a flash of lightening in the sky, life passes by; it flows by like a torrent rushing down the mountainside.

The impermanence of everything we perceive with our senses is one of the main causes of our suffering-experience. This world is impermanent, and impermanence is sorrowful. Yet we do not suffer because the things of this world are impermanent, but because we cling to impermanence. Consequently, we do not suffer because the world is not alright but because we are not alright.

Thus it is a question of inwardly letting go, in order to regain everything on a new, higher level. Here we attain a completely new perspective, resulting in freedom and inner detachment from things. However, such real freedom from things can never be achieved by depriving oneself of the things themselves because this does not yet give us freedom as long as we still desire them.

Only by becoming empty and free from our conditioned

projections which we place on things do we let go of our attachments and desires. Through this we retain a non-attaching mind, everywhere and at all times, so that we deal with things in a free, non-identifying way.

This is what really makes us free and empty, even when we possess many things. In the words of the Christian Mystic Meister Eckhart from the fourteenth century:

We should have as though we had not, and yet possess all things.

The Path to Higher Awareness

5

Understanding the nature of the mind

Inner emptiness from all phenomena is the unavoidable prerequisite for experiencing our true being. What hinders our ascent to the Divine, what holds us down and binds us to the dimension of space-time is not our body or external things. Instead, it is our own projections with their resulting entanglements in the diversity of an external world of phenomena.

Yet since the true nature of things is just Mind and thus void, our enchainment to phenomena dissolves of its own accord as soon as we understand the nature of the mind. This means we become free by recognising that the nature of the mind and the nature of the things is one, for everything is the One Mind, besides which nothing else exists. The Vedanta Master Ramana Maharshi, one of the principal spiritual masters of the 20th century, who died in 1950, tells us this too:

> The universe is just an object created by the mind, that exists in the mind. Only our habitude of viewing the world as real and beyond our self hides

our pure, true being.

Everything we perceive and experience is not real but a product of our projecting mind. Thus, the whole external world of phenomena, indeed the entire cycle of birth and death is in reality, nothing other than the product of the working of our mind and not an external experience.

We are convinced that everything we experience, whether it be joy or suffering, is brought about by a real external world. For this reason we believe that all our problems disappear when we alter the external situation according to our conceptions, but this is a great fallacy, which binds to Samsara, the cycle of birth and death. For wherever we go and whatever changes we make externally, we still end up in the same situation every time. The external backdrop on the drama-stage of life has changed, but the drama remains the same.

Yet, when we achieve greater awareness and perceptive clarity through meditation practice, we will recognise that we are the cause of all these experiences under which we suffer. And so we will understand which ways of thinking and behaving are beneficial to our spiritual attainment and happiness, and which ones we must give up in order to reach true liberation.

Letting go of concepts

Each of our actions causes an energetic impulse which reflects back on to its causing factor, this being the one who acts. Thus we always reap exactly what we sow, based on the universal law of Karma, of cause and effect. If we sow the seed of a poisonous plant, we will unavoidably reap poisonous fruits, and the seed of a healing plant will bring forth a plant which has a healing effect.

Whether we like it or not, everything that happens in our lives is the outcome of thought and its resulting actions. The true factor which causes Karma is therefore rather to be found in our thinking, which is clearly the one that takes the decision to act, than in the action itself.

Everything that happens in our lives is the result of decisions we made at some time in the past. The tragedy here is that most people make their decisions unconsciously. We are indeed capable of making an endless number of decisions, yet the majority of people have turned themselves into true bundles of conditioned reflexes. These reflexes are unconscious reactions to external circumstances and the behaviour of other people, which make conditioned people predictable. Most people suffer from this compulsion of behaviour patterns which constantly repeat themselves and their predictable reactions to all sorts of environmental stimuli. Their whole thinking is purely mechanical and their reactions automatic. This means that nothing is alive in them, nothing new, nothing creative, original.

If we wish to liberate ourselves from such a life of imprisonment in the straightjacket of unconscious behaviour patterns, we must firstly gain distance from ourselves. This means that through meditation practise we achieve higher mindfulness, which leads us to make all decisions consciously and without emotions. As a result, we liberate all our habitual behaviour patterns from the realm of the unconscious and raise them to the higher level of crystal clear awareness. Finally, we reach that grade of higher awareness which distinguishes itself through spontaneous, non-conditioned thinking and acting.

Liberation from our entanglement is thus only possible on the path to realisation when we become aware of the voidness and unrealness of all phenomena. This is the only way we can become free of our concepts and identifications which bind worldly people, caught in their ignorance. They are like long-serving prisoners who have become so used to their chains, even taking pleasure in them, that they no longer have a longing for freedom.

Since their mind is overlaid with clouds of ignorance, they can no longer recognise the radiating reality of their true being. And so they seek externally, without knowing what they are seeking, for that which can only be found within. The Mind, as man's innate divine light, is just waiting for ignorance to be eradicated, so that it may radiate forth like the sun once the Maya-clouds have been driven away.

6

The Reality
of our Original Being

In the ocean of the changing world

The more we become aware of the all-embracing wholeness of divine being both within us and beyond us, the less we will be able to believe in the reality and the importance of our personality, limited by our ego-delusion, and an external world it experiences. Yet, whoever lives solely in the illusion of his ego-bound world of thinking and feeling will be thrown about in the ocean of a changing world and remains a slave of his concepts, bound to the wheel of existence. And so he moves unceasingly from birth to birth, possessed by the delusion of countless fantasies as the vacuous illusion of his thinking.

We are like the old beggar who lives in an old, derelict shack and finally dies of hunger, not knowing that there is a great treasure right under his feet. Bodhidharma, the legendary first patriarch of Zen in China from the sixth century depicts this deplorable situation most strikingly:

The people of this world seek buddha far away.

They do not know that buddha is the essence of their own mind.

Furthermore, in the Viveka Chudamani, one of the principal Indian Vedanta scriptures from the ninth century we read:

You are Brahman, divine reality, pure consciousness, the observer of all experiences, and your true being is bliss.

In the depths of our being, we humans are buddha, divine reality. We are that, from out of which everything in the universe has its origin. This means we are nothing other than the One Mind, the eternal, immutable buddha-substance, the original source of the entire cosmos.

Yet sadly, people are unable to perceive the condition of their original Enlightenment because they only take that to be the mind which thinks, feels and perceives. Most of them are even of the opinion that the mind is nothing more than the result of brain activity within the bony shell of their skull. They are entirely convinced that our brain produces the mind by means of complex neurological processes. As such, these materialistic-oriented rationalists view the mind as the result of biochemical processes in the brain cells.

However, in truth it is quite the opposite. The brain is nothing more than a material compaction of spiritual energy, and therefore the mind is not the result, but the actual cause of all being and thus of brain activity too.

Original buddha-essence

The One Mind is the universal ultimate ground at the base of all our experiences. No matter how many sequences of motion take place within it, it nonetheless remains constantly unmoved. Nothing can sully it and nothing can reduce its unending brilliance. For this reason, the Chinese Zen Master Huang-po says:

> Our original buddha-nature is, viewed from the highest truth, devoid of any atom of objectivity. It is void, omnipresent, silent and pure. It is glorious and mysterious peaceful joy – and that is all. Penetrate deeply into it by awakening to it yourself.

As long as we continue to be blinded by our ignorance, we cannot recognise this spiritual gloriousness of our true being. In the identification with the interwoven memories of our old, dead past we have become blind to the reality of our true being. We have become caught in the deep-rooted pattern of memories which sustain our feeling of being a separate entity. This spiritual blindness is the true cause of our attachment in terms of grasping and rejecting. It is this attachment which in turn solidifies our ego-consciousness and thus chains us to the cycle of birth and death.

In this way we are trapped in the realm of deceptive illusions. By identifying with the unreal, we are no longer able to penetrate the deception of our ego-delusion and recall our original state, our buddha-nature.

To this, the following Zen anecdote:

A Zen monk asks Zen Master Wie-kuan, "What is Tao?"

The master replies, "Tao is the reality at the base of everything and is directly before your eyes."

The monk continues, "Why can I not see it then?"

The master says, "Because you are thinking about your 'I'."

The monk, "Can you see it then?"

The master, "As long as you still use words like 'I' and 'you' and use phrases like 'you see' and 'I do not see', you cannot see Tao."

The monk replies confused, "If there is no longer

any I or you, can it then be seen?"

The master, "If there is no longer any I or you, who is going to see it?"

7

The Immortality of the True Self

The illusion of the personality

When we take what we commonly call our human personality and subject it to a thorough analysis, we will discover that its presence is nothing more than illusion. In fact, we will discover that this so-called "personality" is nothing other than a mere collection of elements of existence which are in a constant process of transformation.

These impersonal elements of existence, known in Buddhism as "Skandhas" are: corporeality, sensation, perception, mental formations and consciousness. However, they are inconstant, without substance, and thus they are empty. They do not possess an existence which surpasses death, neither individually nor in combination with one another.

The whole personality is thus made up of nothing other than a chain of moments of existence and combinations in the form of moments of consciousness, each one following the other in rapid succession. The delusion of a separate, individual personality then arises through our identification with these brief moments of consciousness, appearing and dissolving in functional dependency on each other.

However, once we have finally recognised that the elements of existence which make up the delusion of a personality are not our true self, we need not fear their dissolution in death – quite the contrary! The demise of the elements of existence would mean the ascent of the inner light of the one who is free of all identifications.

To this end, the Chinese Zen Master Huang-po gives us the following essential description. One can justifiably say that it is one of the best summaries of Zen teaching.

> If an ordinary man, when he is about to die, could only recognise the voidness of the elements of existence which form the delusion of a personality, and completely grasp that they do not constitute an "I", and could he recognise that the true Mind is formless and is neither coming nor going. That his nature neither commences at birth nor perishes at his death, but is whole and motionless in its very depths, and that the Mind is one with all phenomena, he would receive Enlightenment in a flash.

He would transcend the world and be one with the Absolute. He would achieve the state of pure being. This is the fundamental truth.

The inescapability of death is an undeniable fact. The fact that one day we shall die is the highest certainty, and the highest uncertainty is the hour of death. Everyone knows that at some point they must die, but most people have put the thought far from reach that death could come "now", within the hour.

Yet it is a fact that our life-force can fall as quickly as a dew drop from the tip of a blade of grass. A human life is as easy to destroy as a soap bubble.

At the moment of death

All of a sudden, death can surprise us, whether we are ready for it or not. That is why it is crucial to develop a state of mind which is at all times aware of the uncertainty of the hour of death, for the moment of death is the most important moment in our lives. The state of mind in which we die is ultimately decisive for everything which happens to us in Bardo – the intermediate state between death and rebirth – and thus for the nature of our rebirth too.

To this, let us hear the final words of Zen Master Mjanpu, whose cloister was attacked by robbers in the Sung-Dynasty. When the robbers had decided to kill the old master with the sword, he requested they bring him paper and a writing brush so that he may write down his final words:

Before me lies a joyful event, for today is my lucky day on which I shall enter into the Buddha-paradise of boundless light.
Please fulfil my joy with a stroke of your sword.

Strike me now, what are you waiting for!

Yet most people are afraid of dying. But that is completely unnecessary since the divine Universal Mind; that is: the One Mind, beside which nothing else exists, is thus this dying too. When I die, it is the One Mind itself which transforms in the process of dying into a new state of being.

When I die, my own world dies with me, just as when I was born; my own world was born too. Ultimately, this means that I was not born into a world in space and time which existed before me and therefore, when I die, I will not leave a world behind me. The Chinese Zen Master Han-shan from the seventeenth century expresses this in the following words:

> It is essential to have unshakable belief in the original purity of the Self-Mind. In its consummate infiniteness it entirely fills the whole universe with its brilliance. Primarily there is nothing beyond the One Mind. There is no body, no intellect-consciousness and no world, just as there are no false ideas or thinking, dictated by

emotions.

This truth reveals all forms of illusory, unreal objects. All the manifestations before my eyes are illusions – there are just reflections which appear in the true mind.

The eternal, unchanging self

It is solely a question of perceiving the unreality of the elements of existence which form the delusion of a personality and of having unshakeable trust in the immortality of our true self. It is the trust that in death, an endless horizon will open up to us, so that rather than dying into a void, we will die into the splendour of divine being.

If we perceive the emptiness of body, mind and world at the moment of death, we can pervade everything in perfect clarity, and all identifications and attachments dissolve by themselves.

Then from out of the midst of the darkness of death, the divine light will radiate over us, mysterious and wonderful, and will consume us. We will be transformed into the radiating gloriousness of divine being.

This inexpressible reality, which lies beyond all human thought, is the eternal, unchanging self which forms the basis of everything we experience. In Buddhism, this deathless true self is attested most clearly by Buddha's words:

O monks, there is a thing, unborn, unrealised, in-composite. Were this not so, there would be no escape from the world of the born, the realised, the composite.

We are aware of the fact that our body is mortal and is thus predestined to dissolve one day. Yet this does not pertain to our true self, which neither begins at birth nor dissolves at death and is thus immortal. It is not touched by the changes of the world of phenomena to which this body with all its psychological aspects belongs. In the Upanishads, the holy Indian scriptures we read:

This eternal self is never born nor will it ever die. It comes from nowhere and will not become anything. It is unborn, everlasting, immortal. It does not die when the body dies.

The following words of the Christian Mystic Meister Eckhart sound almost like a commentary to this chapter of the Katha-Upanishad:

... therefore I am the cause of my self according to

my being, which is eternal, but not according to my becoming, which is temporal. And therefore I am unborn, and in the manner in which I am unborn I can never die. In my unborn manner I have been eternally, and am now, and shall eternally remain.

8

The Perpetual Presence of the Self

The experience of our true self

In our entire human life there can be nothing more meaningful or more important than the experience of our true, essential being. Yet although our true self, as our innermost reality, is the true essential core of every being, only very few people are aware of its constant presence.

The eternal presence of our true, birth- and deathless being ultimately means that it can become a vivacious experience for anyone who turns inwards in mystical immersion.

Therefore, the experience of our true self cannot be viewed as something which comes into our lives. Experiencing our true self, as the sense and reason of our whole existence cannot not be anything special, different or abstract but instead, it is real life itself. Indeed, as the eternal original source of all life, it is the life which gives life to all life. It is closer to us than our own heart, closer than our own breath, and as original, pure consciousness, it is the basis of all sensations and perception. As the true nature of the mind it is completely beyond everything that the normal consciousness is able to fathom.

It is absolute reality, existing of itself, which the enlightened masters of all religions have proclaimed for thousands of years. Whether Buddha, Jesus, Lao-tse or Meister Eckhart, one thing was always important to them: that a person awaken from his dream of birth and death and experience his true, divine self.

We all live in direct unity with our true, divine self – nothing could be closer. As the reality existing of itself, it is constantly present at the core of each person. If a person is not aware of this, it is just because he has lost himself, blinded by the fascination of external things, in the illusion of body, mind and world. In the words of the Christian Mystic Meister Eckhart:

God is within, but we are without; God is at home within us, but we are far away.

The eternal source of all life

Our true, divine self is constantly present but only very few are interested in it, unless that is, through positive karma or experiences of suffering in their lives, they be-come aware of the impermanence of human existence and within them, the longing for the Eternal and Imperi-shable awakens.

In our whole lives there is only really one necessity: the experience of our birth- and deathless true self. As long as we do not experience this it is not possible to find true happiness and contentment. Regardless of what we achieve, be it riches, honour or power, the feeling will always remain that something essential is missing.

By not recognising the perpetual presence of his divine self, a person turns away from the source of all life. This turning away from the divine source is also a turning away from the Absolute to non-being, from life to death. Yet whoever slumbers as a walking corpse in separation from the original source of all life in moronic, apathetic unawareness, cannot hope to enter into the fullness of the Great Life at the moment of his death.

Lost in the labyrinth of their self-created problems, peo-ple of today have become caught in a tremendous sum of conflicts which threaten to overwhelm them. Indeed, due to our lack of true self-perception we have separa-ted ourselves from the all-embracing wholeness of being and experience ourselves as individuals, separated from all other beings. Due to this dualistic perspective we constantly try to stabilise our pseudo "I", concentrate solely on our egoistic self-interests and judge others. In this way a great deal of attachment and rejection arises, which in its turn, creates negative karma and endless suffering for ourselves and others.

Thus, a solution to all our self-created problems can only come when we liberate ourselves from the illusion of separation and perceive our true self as the common self of all beings.

For when the same self is the heart of the selfhood of every individual, there can be no distinct individual, existing of its own accord. There can be no distinct personality, just as there can be no wave on the surface of the ocean which distinguishes itself from all other waves.

Everything is the one ocean in its all-embracing wholeness and equally, everything is the One Mind, our true self, beside which nothing else exists.

The fleetingness of life

The real root of all human suffering is the non-perception of our true essence. Regardless of what we have achieved in this life – it is no use to us at the moment of our death and will dissolve away. Thus when we spend our whole lives, right up to the moment of death in our blindness for the essential, solely with matters of this life, it is a grave misfortune, for we have missed out on the true meaning of life.

An essential base element of all genuine spiritual thinking is the thought of the fleetingness of all that exists. We must look the truth in the eye and make it clear to ourselves how fleeting human life is and how uncertain the hour of death. In addition, according to Asiatic teachings, human birth is extremely rare and only through this is it possible to find liberation from the cycle of birth and death. Yet since you cannot know when you will die and how long it will take until you are born again, if at all, you should begin right away in turning your attention to your true self. Whoever waits until he has more time for it will probably never find the time.

By becoming aware of the volatility and thus suffering of all being, a spiritually-oriented person longs for liberation. He longs for the true experience of Being – for being touched and smitten by the Divine. For him it is about the vivacious experience within him of that which is beyond birth and death – and whose presence he feels in his innermost self. In fact, the presence of intrinsic divine reality at the base of our being draws us to it so much that we are called upon to seek it and to find it in mystical immersion.

In the words of the Chinese Zen Master Hung-chi from the twelfth century:

> In order to experience the reality of Zen in all its profoundness, you must clear your mind and immerse yourself in the silent practice of an inner beholding of your true essence.
>
> When you gain an entirely unimpeded insight into the origin of what is real, the Self-Mind is open, brightly shining, without bounds, without middle and end. Completely whole, radiating with light, it shines through the universe and cuts through past, present and future.

This awakening to our true self is nonetheless no goal that is to be reached – rather it is the living perception of this which is. It is the Essence which has always been there within us since it is what we are in truth.

9

The True Self as the Eternal "I Am"

The original source of all things

Beyond everything that sense and reason can comprehend, the eternal divine light shines within us. Yet what use is it to a person when within his own self, he lacks receptiveness for the Divine, with the result that he becomes more and more entangled in the creeping snarl of his spiritual confusion.

But just as a golden chalice can be covered in dirt, without losing any of its true essence, so too lies the true Self inwardly concealed and remains eternally untouched by the dirt of ignorance which covers it.

As long as we still cling to impermanence through our identification with external phenomena, we cannot experience our true state of the unlimited, transmundane Mind. We seek the Eternal in impermanence, without realising that our true being is constantly present in us as the base of all experiences. To this, the Tibetan Mahamudra Master Padmasambhava in the eighth century gives us the following example:

It is totally impossible to find buddha anywhere

other than in one's own consciousness. A person who does not know this may seek externally, but how is it possible to find oneself when one seeks elsewhere than within oneself?

Whoever seeks his own being externally is like a fool who, performing before a crowd, forgets who he is and looks everywhere for himself.

For this reason, Meister Eckhart calls out to us:

Why do you go out? Why do you not remain within yourselves and delve into your own store? Indeed, you carry all truth intrinsically within you!

Zen Master Huang-po too in the ninth century speaks these admonishing words:

Do not bind yourselves to anything beyond the pure buddha-being, the original source of all things.

Since most people live divided from this original source, at the same time they alienate themselves from their true being. It is the self-alienation whose origin arises from a person's ignorance of his true divine nature within him. Thus, liberation from the cycle of birth and death can only be consummated by radically "turning inwards", in a true "Metanoia", an inner return.

The Chinese Zen Master Ta-hui in the twelfth century says this too:

> If you allow your mind to abruptly sink into the unfathomable depths which intellect and thought can never penetrate, you will behold the absolute, radiating One Mind. This is how you achieve liberation from the cycle of birth and death.

The eternal "I am"

When a person immerses himself in his inner ground, and his ego and all things are extinguished within him, he will then become that which he seeks. He will recognise himself as the one "who Is" – whose Beingness is within and out of himself.

The ultimate mystery of all being is experienced within us in the absoluteness of our self as the eternal "I Am", which we perceive in the depths of our own being. It is pure being before all that exists, since its essence emanates from out of itself and is not derived from any other essence. In the words of the Chinese sage Lao-tse, the Chinese founding father of Taoism from the sixth century B.C:

There is a being, intangible, sublime.
It precedes heaven and earth,
so silent, so formless.
Alone in itself, unchanging,
all-pervading, everlasting.
Concealed it may be,

yet constantly present.
It appears as the origin
of the myriad beings.

This "I Am" is the reality in everything that is. It is pure being, the eternal original source from which all life flows in never-ending abundance. As the source of all consciousness, it is the consciousness in all things, and whoever perceives it experiences the whole of creation as this "I Am".

Once we have finally awakened to this our indwelling divineness, all being has been transformed. We have returned to the source of all life such that we dwell in constant awareness of our fundamental Heart-Mind.

Just like the wise seer at the close of the Taittiriya-Upanishad we can then call out:

How wonderful! "I Am", before even the gods appeared. I am the centre and the source of immortality and I radiate like the sun.

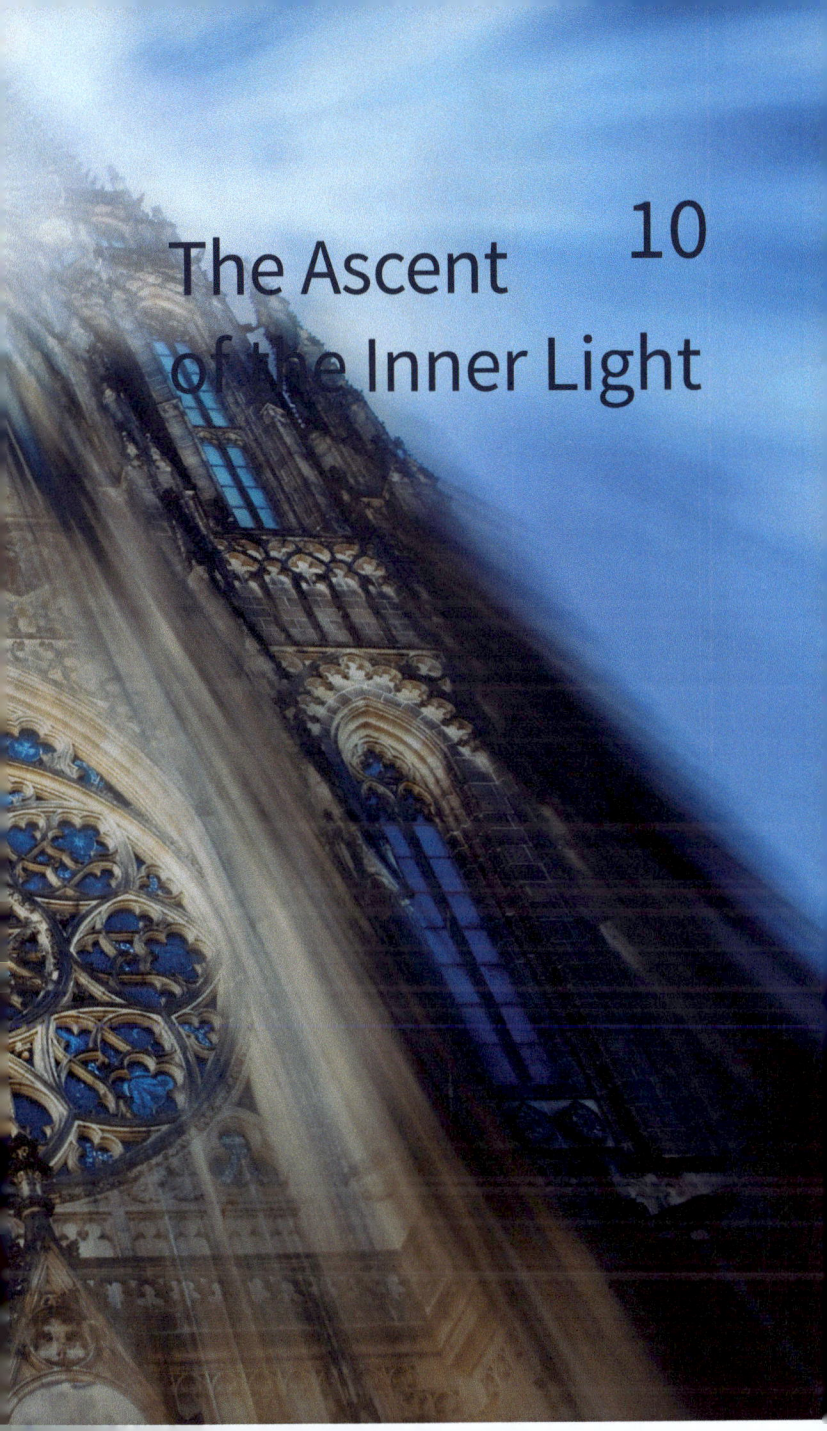

The Ascent
of the Inner Light

10

Mystical death

The process of dying into the dark abyss of divine nothingness as experienced in mystical death is an awakening to ultimate reality. The ego or "I" vanishes in the "dark night of the senses and the mind", and the true self witnesses its resurrection in the eternal splendour of its original being.

In the search for divine being, the soul must lose itself. As paradox as it may seem: we can only experience our true self when there is no longer anyone there who can experience it. For the true self will only unfold when at the moment of mystical death, the false "I" dies, that is, when the delusion of an individual personality dies.

Only when it has truly become night in us will the inner sun of perception arise. The greater the darkness, the brighter the light which shines in us. In the words of the Chinese Zen Master Hui-neng, the sixth patriarch of Zen from the eighth century:

When Prajna, the transcendental wisdom, shines within with its light, and pervading both inner and outer, enlightens them, you will perceive your own mind. When you have perceived your own mind as the One Mind, beside which nothing else exists, you will have achieved great liberation.

The enlightened masters of all times and cultures tell of this unborn "divine light which shines in the darkness". The Indian Vedanta Master Shankara from the ninth century, who is seen as one of most significant advocates of Advaita-Vedanta, speaks of this too:

Just like darkness vanishes in light, its opposite, so does the false "I" vanish with its world of illusion when the light of Brahman – divine reality – rises in the heart. When the deceptive shroud falls, whoever perceives Brahman will become Brahman himself.

The cave of the heart

Yet as long as the superficial-sensory aspect of the external world of phenomena still demands the special interest of the human consciousness, people will remain bound through themselves. For the inner light is concealed by a veil of ignorance caused by the dark clouds of discriminating thought. For this reason, the Chinese Zen Master Huang-po calls out to us:

> The Mind is filled with radiating clarity. Therefore, cast off the darkness of your old concepts. Free yourselves of everything!

The inexpressible mystery of God's birth at the base of the soul will only reveal itself to us once all external and internal compulsions – that is: all behaviour patterns and mind-sets – have been completely discarded. This inner base of the soul is man's innermost core – the centre of our being, the origin of all life. It is the "cave of the heart", in which the light of our true being lights up the entire universe like the sun, and reveals itself to us in the

mysterious beholding of the hidden depths. Impenetrable for the senses and the intellect, it is the radiating gloriousness of Atman, our true self. In the Chandogya-Upanishad it is written:

This light, which shines higher than the heavens, above all worlds, beyond everything, higher than the highest worlds, is this same light which shines deep within Man. In unending darkness, within the heart, the ascent of the inner light will be bestowed upon us at the moment of mystical death. The Chinese Zen Master Huang-po speaks too of the sudden blaze of divine light as the Eternal in Man:

If you would finally throw off all conceptual thought in an instant, your true essence would manifest itself like the sun ascending through the void and illuminating the whole universe without hindrance or bounds.

The radiating light of reality

The "Great Death", as it is known in Zen, becomes the "Great Resurrection". As paradox as it may sound, the death and demise of the clasping little "I" is the ascent of the true self. What we experience in the process of mystical death as dying, manifests itself as the transition from death to life. We witness our resurrection from the realm of the dead.

It is the great moment of awakening from the dream of a supposed world of multiplicity. By breaking through to our true being we are raised above all limitations of an earthly-bound human existence and we experience our ascent above the dark haze of phenomena into the clear light of reality.

The wall of death has been penetrated, the veil of Maya tears and reveals the radiating light of our true self.

Wherever a person is prepared to totally abandon himself out of love of the Divine, in complete relinquishment of his self, he will be granted the ascent of the inner light. Symeon the New Theologian, doubtlessly the most significant Christian mystic of the Greek Orthodox

Church, was one of those who was prepared to completely surrender himself:

> Suddenly I felt that He was within me. In the middle of my heart he appeared like the light of the circular sun disk.
> And the light raises me above everything, and I, who was in the midst of all things, now dwell outside of everything, I know not if beyond my body too. Now in truth I am completely here, where "He" is solely light and simply is.

11

Returning to
the Origin of all Being

God and I are one

Beyond everything that sense and reason can comprehend we shall perceive reality. We will become one with the unending mystery by dying into the dark abyss of divine nothingness which manifests itself as the radiating plenitude of divine being.

The Christian mystic Dionysius Areopagita extols the blazing light of divine darkness as follows:

> O darkness of silence! It would not suffice to say of you, you shine like pure darkness in radiating light, nor to say of you, your resplendence remains ever unchanged; nor would it suffice to say of you, you dazzle the darkness of the ultimate ground to the point of bursting with the brilliance of your plenitude and that you are more beautiful than beauty itself.

When divine reality bursts into the life of a person who yearns for God, he who has reached Enlightenment can no longer say, "I have seen God." He cannot even say, "I was one with God," but just, "God and I are completely one." In the words of Jesus in the Gospel according to John, "The Father and I are one". The wise seer in the Katha Upanishad speaks of this too:

> Only the pure of heart can fathom the mystery of immortality when immersed in deep contemplation, he perceives: The Self within me and Brahman are one. I am Brahman and Brahman is me. Being One with God is immortality.

The one who experiences, the experience and that which is experienced become completely one. In the words of Meister Eckhart:

> If God is to be seen, it must take place in a light which is God himself. The eye with which I see God is the same eye with which God sees me – my eye and God's eye is one eye, one perception and one being.

However, well aware of the exceptional nature of his utterance, Meister Eckhart adds:

As long as a person is not akin to this truth, so long will he be unable to understand these words. For this is a bare truth which comes directly from God's heart.

Instant Enlightenment

The awakening to ultimate reality is something that is always beyond all human capability. The Enlightenment experience always remains a divine gift of grace. At least this is how it is felt by those who are literally overwhelmed by this experience and struck to the core of their being. They realise: I myself am not the cause of the experience but rather, I am the one who is smitten.

Hence, for the most part, the Enlightenment experience is fulfilled in a moment outside of normal meditation and constantly then, when it is not expected. For example, some are granted Enlightenment quite suddenly and unexpectedly whilst quietly abiding in the countryside. At the precise moment when we relax and let go, or to put it better – have become this letting-go ourselves – everything will be bestowed upon us.

For others it happens whilst reading a passage from a religious text, even though they may have already read the same verse many times before without their spiritual eye opening. Often it is just a sound, a bell, a bird call, the sight of a leaf falling from a tree, or a flower which can become the direct impulse.

Thus for the well-known Zen poet Bassho from the seventeenth century, the trigger of great Enlightenment was the sound of a frog leaping while he was sitting by the old pond in the cloister garden. Hereupon he wrote his famous Zen-poem – a Haiku:

> Old pond, a froglet leaps into water,
> a sound – plop!

The Japanese Zen Master Imakita Kôsen from the nineteenth century gives us the following impressive description of his sudden Enlightenment experience:

> One night, it was suddenly as though the boundary between earlier and later had been cut. I entered into the marvellous realm of wondrousness. I was at the heart of the "Great

Death", no perception of the existence of all things or of myself remained. All that I felt was how a spirit in my body grew to ten thousand worlds and an endless blaze of light arose.

Baptism by fire of the mind

The Enlightenment experience is the great turning point in a person's life, which touches his whole being at its innermost core. He experiences a spiritual revolution, a tremendous "baptism by fire of the mind" onto the highest level of awareness of the all-encompassing universal consciousness. For, in this rebirth he has reached a new and entirely different state of being which radically changes his whole perspective and attitude to life. This experience does not only influence his mental attitude to things, rather it transforms his whole consciousness into a profound and all-encompassing understanding of life.

A person who has awoken to the true nature of the Mind dwells beyond birth and death, such that the question of "To be or not to be" has lost its meaning for him. He no longer has any reason to cling to life. Since he has recognised the wonderful unity of life and death he is beyond all duality and individual limitation.

He abides in the great affirmation and fullness of life for, through having died into the "mystical death", he has experienced his rebirth as enlightened being from out of the dream of birth and death. His liberation from the shadowy darkness of Maya has transformed his state of obscuration of the mind into the enlightened state of the boundless Transcendent Mind.

He has died and has arisen from the dead. He is the awakened or enlightened one, who has awakened to the clear light of reality. The words of the Gospel according to John are fulfilled in him:

> He will not walk in darkness but will have the light
> of eternal life.

He who has awakened to the birthless and deathless reality of his true self through the experience of Enlightenment witnesses himself as the one who has always existed, and is now the radiating Self-Mind. The birth of God at the base of the soul has become a living experience in him. He experiences himself as unborn and undying and as eternity itself. He has returned to the origin of all being, to the inexhaustible source of all life.

Glossary

Advaita-Vedanta Sanskrit, is one of the three major philosophical, theological systems in Hindu Vedanta. Its main leading exponent was Shankara (ninth century), one of India's greatest sages and philosophers. The Advaita-Vedanta teaches that the divine Universal Mind →Brahman, the Self →Atman and the external world of phenomena are utterly one. In Shankara's Viveka-Chudamani, "The Crest-jewel of Discrimination" it is written, "You are Brahman, pure consciousness, the observer of all experiences, and your true being is bliss."

Atman Sanskrit In Hinduism it is the immortal true self of mankind. As absolute consciousness it is the impartial observer behind all experiences and identical with →Brahman.

Bardo Tibetan, literally: "intermediate state", relates to the intermediate state between death and reincarnation. Buddhist teaching strongly stresses the direction-defining force of the state of mind of a dying person (meaning virtuous, not-virtuous or neutral) and also the negative influences of greed, hate and ignorance during bardo itself.

Brahman Sanskrit, the one, eternal, all-pervading absolute, origin and bearer of the entire universe. The philosophy of Vedanta (→Advaita-Vedanta) teaches that Brahman – the Absolute, surpassing the personal level and →Atman, the true self in all beings are one. Brahman, the sole existing truth, is the essence and the Self (Atman) of all being.

The Viveka-Chudamani, one of the most significant texts of Advaita-Vedanta says: "Atman is one with Brahman. This is the highest truth: Only Brahman is real. There is nothing else besides it. When it has been recognised as highest reality, there exists nothing else besides Brahman." This insight that Brahman and Atman are one is regarded as the highest goal, since it brings liberation from the imprisonment in →samsara, the cycle of birth and death.

Buddha Sanskrit, literally: "the awakened one". 1. The historical Buddha Shakyamuni, who was born in India in ca. 563 B.C. 2. A person who has fulfilled complete Enlightenment (→satori), liberating him from the cycle of birth and death (→samsara). 3. The final truth, the true nature of all being.

Buddha-Dharma Sanskrit (Jap. Buppo), "buddha-law". The teachings of the historical Buddha Shakyamuni. In Zen however, we do not denote buddha-dharma as the teaching that can be conveyed in words, rather it is the highest truth, which is inaccessible for discriminating, conceptual thinking. It is that essential truth which led to Buddha's teachings and which can only be conceived in direct comprehension, in the experience of Enlightenment (→satori).

Buddha-Nature Skt., "Buddhata", the true nature of all beings, which makes it possible for a person to reach Enlightenment (→satori).
Dharma Sanskrit, a term with various meanings. The teachings of →Buddha. Universal order and its laws. In this book, mainly used in the sense of the teachings of Zen.

Dharmakaya Sanskrit, "Body of the great Order". The indescribable true being of the →buddhas, and at the same time, the essence of the universe.

Karma Sanskrit, literally: "Action or deed". The law of cause and effect, by which all thoughts and actions have a corresponding consequence. Through this we determine the quality of our own lives and influence that of others.

Mahamudra Sanskrit, "Great symbol". The principle teaching of the Kagyu school of Tibetan Vajrayana Buddhism. Mahamudra is also translated as the "great seal". This thus expresses the significance of finality, as with a seal. Similar to the practise of Dzogchen in the Nyingma line, Mahamudra practise is about directly perceiving the light-nature of the Mind and thus reaching Enlightenment (→Satori).

Maya Sanskrit, literally: "Illusion, semblance, deception". In Vedanta philosophy (→Vedanta) Maya is the power of great illusion. It veils one's view so that one is unable to recognise →Brahman, ultimate reality. Shankara links Maya to Avidya, ignorance. Ignorance, that is, non-perception of the ultimate reality of Brahman, creates the delusion of an external world of phenomena in space and time by means of its obscurement. Mahayana Buddhism characterises Maya as a deception or illusion, just like a phantasm created by a mirage. Individual things are provisory and have no existence of their own, they are in fact void (Shunyata) and mere conception.

Prajna Sanskrit, literally: "Wisdom" (Pali: Panna, Jap. Hannya). In Mahayana Buddhism Prajna is intuitively experienced insight into the voidness (Shunyata) of all phenomena. Prajna is one of the principle characteristics of Buddhahood.

Samsara Sanskrit, literally: "roaming". The cycle of birth and death. The aim of all Buddhists and Hinduists is liberation from samsara, and thus from suffering. It is liberation from the imprisonment in the wheel of – birth, ageing, despair, illness, pain and death.

Satori Jap. (Chin. Wu). Zen term for the experience of Enlightenment, or awakening. Satori is far more than an intuitive understanding of true being, as in the experience of Kensho, since the person who experiences Satori dissolves entirely into it. In Zen, Satori is described as the rebirth of the true self once the false, illusory self; the ego-delusion has died the "Great Death".

Upanishads Sanskrit: Upanishad, literally: "to sit close by", i.e. to sit near to the master to receive the secret teachings. The Upanishads are a category of texts which make up the final part of the Veda and are the fundamental basis of →Advaita-Vedanta. They are concerned with ultimate truth and belong to the holy revelation scriptures of Hinduism.

Vedanta Sanskrit Advaita-Vedanta

ZEN-ZENTRUM
TAO 道禅 CHAN

Tao Chan Zentrum e.V.
Gemeinnütziger Verein
Germany

The Tao-Chan Zen Centre is under the personal direction of Zen Master Zensho W. Kopp.

During his many years as an active spiritual master, a large community of students have come together whom he regularly instructs.

Zen-Day

Twice a month, the Tao-Chan Zen Centre organises an open Zen-day, led by Zen Master Zensho W. Kopp.

Information and registration
Tel. +49 (0)611 940 623-1 Fax -2
www.tao-chan.org
www.facebook.com/ZenZentrumTaoChan

Books by Zen Master Zensho W. Kopp

All books available at: www.tao-chan.org

The Freedoom of Zen
*The Zen book that shatters
all limits and bounds*

ISBN 978-3751937-01-6

True Life Through Zen
*Spiritual self-realisation
in daily life*

ISBN 978-3-734743-55-9

**Words of the
Awakened Mind**
*Aphorisms of a
Western Zen Master*

ISBN 978-3-848241-34-7

Lao-tse – Tao Te King
The Book of Tao and
Spiritual Force

Transcription by Zen Master
Zensho W. Kopp

ISBN 978-3-842328-61-7

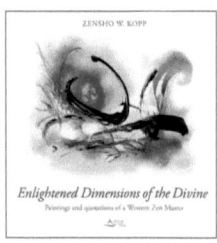

**Enlightened Dimensions
of the Divine**
*Paintings and quotations of
a Western Zen Master*

ISBN 978-1-4827-9942-2

Living in inner fullness
*Aphorisms of a
Western Zen Master*

ISBN 978-3-751935-09-8

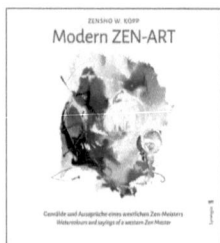

Modern ZEN-ART
*Watercolours and sayings of a
Western Zen Master*

ISBN 978-3-907246-09-2

DE /EN